LAUREATE SERIES

MUSIC MINUS ONE
ADVANCED
CONTEST SOLOS

TROMBONE
MUSIC BOOK

PERFORMANCE GUIDE
COMMENTARY BY JAY FRIEDMAN

CORELLI
Sonata in G Minor — *Adagio and Allegro*

The Corelli Sonata should be played simply, like Bach. Don't use much vibrato. Just whine into the natural sound of the instrument.

There are many suspensions which should be emphasized. When ever you have a note tied across the bar line, the suspension should be accented and then tapered off. When you come to the cadence, you should relax. The kind of accent here is not the usual kind. Instead of hitting the note with a bang, try to get a very musical, bell-like tone. Not too much tongue; just give the notes to be accented a slight nudge with the breath.

In the *Allegro,* there is no need to play staccato. The eighth notes skip around, and the listener will be aware of the separations even though you play in broad, lyric style. Staccato playing would make the piece too mechanical. Use a gentle vibrato on the half-notes. Be declarative without being too aggressive.

The piano part takes over the figures of moving notes in measure 65. Be sure that the single quarter notes always lead into the dotted half notes. The long notes should be held full value with good sound. Keep your tone light on the last three notes. And no vibrato; just the bare sound of the trombone.

DE LA NUX
Concert Piece

This piece encompasses a variety of musical problems, but the predominate feeling is baroque. The beginning is very subdued. Just a light vibrato on the long notes; the moving notes should be smooth and straight.

The intensity increases at letter A. Use more vibrato, and play the *forte* nice and full, with a feeling of *tenuto.*

I prefer the upper notes at letter B because I like the big jump—F down to G. It's more interesting. But be careful of the sound quality on the low notes!

The cadenza at letter C should begin a little on the slow side. Be sure to differentiate between the sixteenth notes and the triplets. Play the sixteenth notes before the trill staccato, and then do the trill so fast that the upper note isn't heard clearly. You must feel the rhythm in the 6/4 Allegro. It is difficult to keep moving. The trombone carries on a contrapuntal conversation with the piano. Watch the accents, and play measure 62 a little *marcato.*

The pianist has the more interesting line at letter D. Play it a little slower (check the metronome marking), and give the piano an orchestral backing.

Be sure you get the right tempo at letter E, or the triplets will not sound musical. Don't rush 'em! Play lightly so you don't bog down with your tongue. (I like to play staccato through the entire section marked *Pressez.*) There are some very high skips before letter F, and then a low G which must be nice and strong, so think ahead!

The quarter-note triplets in letter F must be smooth and legato. I use a vibrato on the first two notes of letter F, and no vibrato on the next two. This adds to the interest, and gives a pure, chorale-like feeling to the resolution. The last notes are played with what I call *marcato-tenuto* style. This is basically an orchestral style, not much used in solo work, but very effective in this case. Each note should be long and solid, but should not sting. Give more air than tongue.

ROUSSEAU
Piece Concertante

This piece starts out very simply, in a sort of Bach style. The figures in measures 17 and 19 are rather difficult. They just rely on the breath to make them come out. And that's the only way that you can make them sound nice and smooth.

Another difficult passage begins in bar 52, where you have to use the fourth position for the D-natural. Even though this passage is marked *piano,* the air stream has to be very intense.

Keep the air very strong on the long crescendo which ends on the high C, and use an intense vibrato throughout.

The *Larghetto* should be very songful and melodic. There is a little cadenza-type passage in measure 93 which should be very smooth.

Be sure to articulate the first notes clearly. In bar 95 you have a piano phrase that's sort of an echo-answer. The phrase comes again, followed by another pianissimo echo-answer. You should try to get that kind of effect. When the crescendo begins, give it a lot of vibrato, and let it build up to an intense high A. Notice the marking in measure 110, molto agitato. The music becomes more and more impassioned until you end up *fortissimo.* The low F-sharp in measure 125 should be a nice, big, fat sound, so plan ahead for it!

The cadenza begins with another low F-sharp. It should not be too hard. Play it like an organ note: pedally, deep, and rich. And then play the cadenza with verve!

In measure 152 the beginning is recapitulated, and you have to start building towards the ending. The triplets are difficult, but keep them light and keep them moving. You will have to stay nice and flexible to get up to all the high notes. And good luck on the trill. You'll just have to get it!

Jay Friedman

TUNING
Before the piano accompaniment begins you will hear four tuning notes, followed by a short scale and another tuning note. This will enable you to tune your instrument to the record.

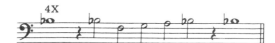

SONATA IN G MINOR
II

ARCANGELO CORELLI
Trans. by Allen Ostrander

Side A - Band 5 ♩ = 60 (2'05")

8058

III

Side A – Band 6 ♩ = 126 (2'25")
Side A – Band 7 ♩ = 96 (2'46")

ARCANGELO CORELLI
Trans. by Allen Ostrander

Allegro moderato

8058

CONCERT PIECE

Side B - Band 1 (2'58")

P. V. DE LA NUX

8058

Allegro—Band 2: 4 beats precede music ♩.=52 (2'12")
Band 3: 6 beats precede music ♩=104 (3'06")

8058

10

8058

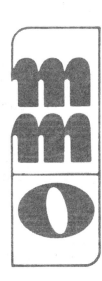

PIECE CONCERTANTE

Side B - Band 4 (6'15")

Side B - Band 5 (7'27")

SAMUEL ROUSSEAU

8058

LS LAUREATE SERIES

MUSIC MINUS ONE 50 Executive Boulevard • Elmsford New York 10523-1325